The Emergency Hustle

The Emergency Hustle

*10 fast cash generating ventures
for hands-on guys and gals*

Demetrius S. Brown

Library of Congress Control Number: 2010916742
ISBN: Softcover   978-1-4568-1370-3
                 Ebook   978-1-4568-1371-0

DISCLAIMER
Nothing illustrated, referenced or written in this guide is to be considered, in any way, as a "guarantee of income". These ventures are suggestions, reminders and information designed to help our readers gauge several avenues of possible income.

This book was printed in the United States of America.

To order additional copies of this book, contact:
Xlibris Corporation
1-888-795-4274
www.Xlibris.com
Orders@Xlibris.com
89917

Contents

Guide edition revised 06/2010

Introduction

Most of the ventures listed in the following pages will actually cost around $10.00 to get started. Many are a revisit to some of the old, simple money-making ideas, we all as kids, or teenagers used at one time or another to earn extra money for the week-end. There are a few new ones since then of course, and there are a few ventures obviously for older teens or adults only. **Most of these one-man ventures are based around curb painting. It's the doorway to all 9 other options listed.**

These are difficult economic times for a lot of people. Some of us face added hardships unless we somehow supplement our income by a few hundred extra bucks a month or a week. Yet, how to do so without incurring ridiculous start-up cost or a substantial investment in time and equipment, or worse, having to pick-a second job, even if it's part-time. If you are an adult or teen who wants to earn extra cash, and do not have a problem with going door-to-door, then give me 16 hours of your time. I'll divide that 16 hours in a way that will demonstrate the way to that extra income.

Depending on your need, you may be able to employ some of these suggestions and earn that extra $200.00, $300.00 or even $400.00 or more a week depending on your choice of ventures. This is designed to be a temporary source of income as long as the season last or until you call it quits. I have personally used all of the opportunities myself, and they work!! My most successful venture was from curb painting. I have devoted a good number of pages to this venture and subject.

None of these projects are new. You can find these same offers and descriptions in dozens of books, manuals and guides. The difference is;

I'll show you how to spend as little as $10.00 to get you started.

It is possible to get a substantial amount of money from this but, it's only designed to be a 200.00, 300.00 or 400.00 weekly supplement to your income. If you can make it more, that's great and I say
"GO FOR IT"!!!!!

Good-Luck and let's get started . . . .

Demetrius S. Brown
Author

A

YOU MAY NOT GET RICH, BUT . . . .

*   *   *

You may not get rich, but then again, who knows?

For now, that lofty goal is on the shelf . . . let's look at some realistic options that can put some extra money in your pocket very quickly. I have had the unpleasant experience of desperately needing some form of immediate cash generation that didn't require weeks or months to start . . . What I needed was a super-cheap way to bring in cash while initially spending as little as possible. Since available cash was so limited, I had to consider some things (like curb painting) that are generally *not* considered by a lot of people as a second source of income . There are probably several occasions when you may see some school or church groups sponsoring these events, but nobody really thinks of it as a credible or consistent money maker. To some degree, they are correct in that, it is seasonal and the end of the season is also the end of the income from that particular venture.

B

SHORT-TERM-QUICK CASH

This is what we call the "Emergency Hustle", also known as a "Mini-Venture" or the "$10.00" venture. Simply stated, in the short-term, many of the items you are going to use for a couple of these ventures will be simple household items and a little resourcefulness. It could be about 6 or 7 days before you will be able to collect your first (Quick-Cash) earnings and discard the homemade items for better supplies. Naturally, we will need a few store items, but with the advent of discount stores, dollar stores and the like, we can minimize our out of pocket expenses tremendously. The "quick-work" supplies listed below apply to Curb and/or lot painting specifically.

C

QUICK-WORK SUPPLIES

1 Set of oil board 3" or 4" alpha-numeric stencils (6 to 8 inch stencils should be used if painting a Parking lot)
1 Roll of 2" or 3" shipping/ masking tape (usually beige in color)
Some old house cloths or clean rags and an old (or new) Back-pack
Paint scraper
Box cutter, sharp knife or other similar cutting tool
1 can of spray paint—Black (Flat black is best, although semi-gloss can also be used, avoid enamel)
1 can of spray paint—White* (Flat or semi-gloss) *If your funds will allow it, buy a gallon
Small container of ordinary dishwashing liquid (used for fresh paint spills)
Multi-pack of paint brushes (a 3 pack will do, but make sure the brushes are 1", 2" and 3")
Wire brush (The block type made of hard plastic or wood is good. Even better if it has the centered, screwhole for attaching to a handle).

Small hand held Wisk broom
Clipboard, pen, paper and Receipt book
Gloves (either rubber, latex or cloth . . . as long as you can function)
Hand cleaner and water for washing up
Drinking Water (working on concrete, asphalt and cement on a hot day can dehydrate you very quickly).

I

Curb Address Painting

A. Excellent Weekly Money Maker

Of the 10 options listed in this guide, none is perhaps more lucrative than curb painting. It is free advertisement for everything else you may want to try, and it allows you to take advantage of the fact that you already have broken the ice as far as contact and communication. This is also a very old method of earning income. We used to do this when I was in the Cub Scouts in 1959. It was how we earned extra money for group outings and such. (Oops! I just gave away my age). Curb painting is a job that often leads to other work and usually with the same customers who had their curb painted. Think about it, these folks you are meeting at their door, work in all kinds of industries and professions. You never know what the result will be when you knock on someone's door. So let's get the bottom line on our first $10.00 venture; curb painting.

B. Types of curbs

There are *2 basic types of curbs: Slopes and standard. *(See photo illustration pg. 8)

Standard curbs are the ones we see everyday . . . edge of the sidewalk and then vertically straight down to the street. While you can charge more for standard curbs, they take much longer to do.

A sloping or angled curb is just that, a curb that can be convex or concave. It is a continuous single piece with no edges that starts at the top of the sidewalk and gently slopes downward to the street. The good part about sloping curbs: They're easy to do, and it takes very little time to do it. That's important because at around $8.00 to $10.00 each, they become a real money-maker. No training per say, is required, just a little practice. Do your own curb for self-training.

I've done them at a rate of approximately 1 address every 6 minutes. At that rate, knocking out ten or fifteen of these will give you between 100.00 and 150.00 if you charge the maximum rate ($10.00) **, in just over an hour. You can charge as much or as little as you want, but if you charge <u>more</u> than $10.00, you probably won't get the business, you'll just price yourself right out of the market. I charged 7.50 and usually had about 30-35 curbs every Saturday. 30-35 sloping curbs is about the maximum a person working alone can do. We will discuss adding others for greater numbers later.

C. Soliciting Options and Areas

You will need to go door-to-door in residential neighborhoods for about 2 hours each evening, between 5:30pm and 7:30pm, Mon-Thur. It's an optimal time to gather your addresses. Unless you are going to small businesses, I would avoid going door to door during the day as this has proven to be unprofitable because most people are not home. **(It is however, an excellent time to paint).** Some blocks have as little as 4 or 5 houses, usually in a Cul-De-Sac, while other blocks in the same neighborhood, are very long and could have as many as 65 or more. Starting out, stick with the residential neighborhoods, it's the best area to accumulate a large number of customers right away.

**Starting out, it is best to have a lower price than 10.00 on sloping curbs. There are competitors out there more than willing to undercut your price.

D. Weather & Seasonal Limitations

Depending on where you live, your curb painting venture could be limited to the simple change of seasons. Example: if you live in Arizona, Nevada,

New Mexico or Southern California, you can probably get at least 10 out of 12 months to operate. If you live in Oregon or the State of Washington, you may only get 3, 3 ½ or possibly 4 months because of the rainy climate there.

East Coast residents can operate starting in late Spring, and continue through mid-Autumn, pausing on rainy days.

Regardless of where you live, you are at the *mercy* of the *elements*. Nothing can kill productivity like rain. It not only stops you from starting, but forces you to wait until the ground is dry enough for painting. Since you paint outdoors and only paint during the daylight hours, a morning, mid-morning or early afternoon rain can pretty much ruin your day, or in the least, substantially reduce your profits, up to half.

Another of Nature's ordinarily pleasant occurrences is the wind. A strong or consistent wind can cause dirt and other debris to adhere to your wet paint making it look dirty and unprofessional. It also causes a greater degree of overspray. **Caution should be used here;** if it is a windy painting day, try to always position yourself for deflection, so the wind carries your overspray away from any parked vehicles. **You would be liable for any paint damage the overspray may cause**. If at all possible, ask the car owner(s) to move their car *temporarily* to avoid the problem. You will find most vehicle owners are very cooperative since they don't want any damages to their car either. Sometimes though, it's a stranger's car and no one knows who owns it.

E. Hired Help

If you live in a heavily populated area, you may need help. After one or two weeks on your own to accumulate some profits for a good minimal cash flow, you might want to expand a little.

With just one good worker you can triple your profits in one of 2 ways; first, if you use your assistant to help you solicit, you can triple the number of residents signing up for your service. Generally, someone who solicits with you should or could be a valuable partner, if they understand the potential here. It is advisable to make a script for both of you for "consistency of message". If you choose to use your assistant as an employee, you will need to make some pay arrangement, whether it's hourly or commission based. If you decide your helper will paint only, again, you'll need to decide if a flat rate of payment, or percentage of sales is best for both of you. If you have a friend that wants to earn money as badly as you do, you could have a partner, and everything, profits and expenses, get split right down the middle. It could be the beginning of a beautiful relationship.

F. Sales & Net Profit Projections

Take a look at the possibilities! Projections up to 35 customers weekly can be handled by one person, if you gather names during the week and use a single day, like Saturday, to paint. You can do more addresses if you spread out your week and do them daily, using week-ends to collect. Figures are based on an average rate of $8.00 & $10.00 per house. Your actual fee may be more or less, depending on the status and/or class of neighborhood. An economically depressed area forces you to limit your price, whereas well-to-do and other affluent neighborhoods can allow you to charge the max amt of $10 per address/house.

10 homes x 8.00 = $80.00	10 homes x 10.00 = $100.00
15 homes x 8.00 = $120.00	15 homes x 10.00 = $150.00
20 homes x 8.00 = $160.00	20 homes x 10.00 = $200.00
25 homes x 8.00 = $200.00	25 homes x 10.00 = $250.00
30 homes x 8.00 = $240.00	30 homes x 10.00 = $300.00
35 homes x 8.00 = $280.00 - (maximum for single painter)	35 homes x 10.00 = $350.00
40 homes x 8.00 = $320.00	40 homes x 10.00 = $400.00
45 homes x 8.00 = $360.00	45 homes x 10.00 = $450.00
50 homes x 8.00 = $400.00	50 homes x 10.00 = $500.00
55 homes x 8.00 = $440.00	55 homes x 10.00 = $550.00
60 homes x 8.00 = $480.00	60 homes x 10.00 = $600.00
65 homes x 8.00 = $520.00	65 homes x 10.00 = $650.00
70 homes x 8.00 = $560.00 - (maximum for 2 painters)	70 homes x 10.00 = $700.00

Beyond 70 homes, you will probably need a 3rd person, if you are only painting one day a week. This however, does illustrate the earnings potential of such a simple service. If you are fortunate enough to live in a major city, like New York, Philadelphia, Boston, Miami, Chicago, Detroit, or San

Francisco, you will have a long term supply of customers. Midsized cities are also good. Basically, as long as there are paved streets, you will always have business.

Be sure to ask any resident of the block, if they have a Home-owners or community or block organization or group who could represent all interested residents for a "group rate" discount for X numbers of guaranteed home addresses to paint.

G. Sample Scripts

I've included a couple of very basic sales scripts to act as a guide until you create your own.

Sample Script #1 (Always take a few steps back from the door after ringing bell/knocking, its less intimidating)

"Good evening, my name is _____. This *week* we are in your area painting and repainting the worn out curb addresses on your block. We will be painting all *week* and would like to ask if you wish your address to be added to our paint list. You do not pay in advance and collections will be made on either Friday evening between 6:00pm and 8:30pm or Saturday morning, between 9:00am & 12 Noon. Once added to our list, we will paint or repaint your address at some point during the *week*, but won't be by to collect until one of the 2 specified collection times. Again, no advanced payment is required and no one is required to be home. **"May we add your address to the list?"**

Pause and wait for reply, usually, "How much". Friday collections are for any and all addresses completed between Monday –Thursday. It is also a good time to visit any home on the block whose occupants were not home earlier during the week. You may wish to include them for the current week and work a little on Saturday or schedule them for the up coming week. Saturday collections are usually for the remainder of your listed homes completed on Friday. During the collections phase, **mention any other service you offer or are willing to do,** like Venetian blind cleaning, debris removal, gutter cleaning, lawn care, etc. Homes not displaying a painted curb address should also be asked. Any home with a "no soliciting" sign should be skipped, unless you can catch the residents **OUTSIDE** the home.

This is a good opportunity for you to gain more business, albeit different work.

Sample Script #2

"Hello, my name is _____. Saturday, this coming Saturday, *the date* . We will be on your block painting and repainting the worn curb addresses here. You do not pay in advance and we will not collect until after your block is finished Saturday afternoon, and again Sunday morning between 9am and 12 noon. We wanted to know if we can add your address to the list. We charge $_____ and if you think you may not be around, we gladly accept personal checks, which you can just leave in an envelope, or with a neighbor if so choose. **May we add your address to the list?**

++Page 7 is a sample of a typical paint list, Page 8 is an illustration of curb types and driveway boarders. You may copy and use either or both. Modify name, price, etc. as needed.

MASTER PAINT LIST

CURB ADDRESSES   * FOR WEEK OF: __/__/__ to __/__/__

$ 8.00 ea.

	NAME	ADDRESS	INSTRUCTIONS	CMPLT / PAID/ RTN
1.		/	/	/ / /
2.		/	/	/ / /
3.		/	/	/ / /
4.		/	/	/ / /
5.		/	/	/ / /
6.		/	/	/ / /
7.		/	/	/ / /
8.		/	/	/ / /
9.		/	/	/ / /
10.		/	/	/ / /
11.		/	/	/ / /
12.		/	/	/ / /
13.		/	/	/ / /
14.		/	/	/ / /
15.		/	/	/ / /
16.		/	/	/ / /
17.		/	/	/ / /
18.		/	/	/ / /
19.		/	/	/ / /
20.		/	/	/ / /
21.		/	/	/ / /
22.		/	/	/ / /
23.		/	/	/ / /
24.		/	/	/ / /
25.		/	/	/ / /
26.		/	/	/ / /
27.		/	/	/ / /
28.		/	/	/ / /
29.		/	/	/ / /
30.		/	/	/ / /
31.		/	/	/ / /
32.		/	/	/ / /
33.		/	/	/ / /
34.		/	/	/ / /
35.		/	/	/ / /

* PAINT DATES MAY BE CHANGED IN THE EVENT OF INCLEMENT WEATHER.

PLEASE MAKE CHECKS PAYABLE TO: _____

Standard Curb:

Good money maker, but time consuming if both sides are numbered. Add 4-to-5 additional minutes for the second stenciling. The advantage is, you can split your pricing on this type of curb and maximize profit. Example: You can charge $8.00 for a side, or offer a bargain savings by doing both sides for just $10.00 or $12.00. Your customer can recognize savings of 50% to 80% off the second number.

Sloping or Angled Curb:
The easiest and quickest type.

Single blocks are the most valued.
It takes very little time to do and can be *__extremely__* profitable, but only if you are able to find enough residential areas with this curb type.

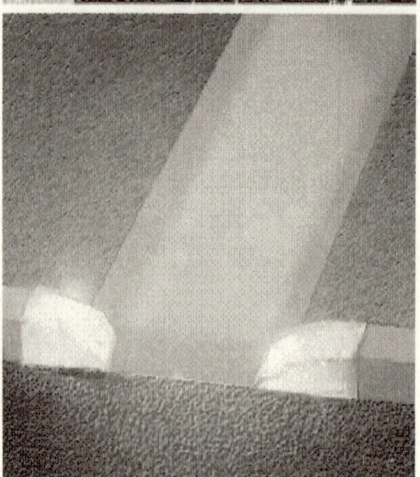

Driveway Boarders:
This is a additional or single sales item. As a single sales item, you can still get between $8.00 to $10.00. As an add-on, I recommend no more than $7.00.

H. Blockers and Painters

For those of you who decide to really go for it and have a partner or at least a potential partner in mind, a description of the function of "blocker" and "painter" is written below.

The **Blocker** is your lead-off person. He or she is the person who paints the rectangular white "block" on the curb in preparation for the numbers painter following behind. The masking tape is used to make your block. The blocker is responsible for graying out of old faded address, if applicable, aligning rectangle so that the white block appears even and straight. Making sure the painting surface is clean, removing any debris, mold, grease, gum, oil or any other foreign matter that could interfere with the paint-to-surface cohesion. Blockers should try to stay 5 or 6 addresses ahead of the painter. If timed right, each "block" your painter gets to, will already be dry and ready for the numbers to be added.

The **Painter** is responsible for the placement of the address numbers themselves. It is his/her responsibility to accurately stencil the numbers onto the freshly painted white block. Painters have to make sure the numbers are properly spaced and even, with minimal overspray. Lop-sided numbers look very tacky and could hurt your efforts. **Remember, each address you paint advertises your business**, so you definitely want your work to look good. A good question to ask your self after stenciling an address is; Would I be okay with this in front of *my* house? The good news for painters is that they are often interrupted by either those folks who were not home during the time you were soliciting on the block, or those who have seen many of their neighbors getting your service and changed their minds.(some people will always be followers). In either case, you will pick-up additional customers as you go through each street.

Don't be afraid to ask for additional business. People are very proud of their homes and offering additional services like driveway borders can add another $4.00 to $7.00 to your sale. This is when you offer appointments for other options like lawn care, or debris removal, gutter cleaning, fish-tank services or Venetian blind cleaning. You are building your customer base at this point and simultaneously listing the versatility of your business.

I. Painting Supplies on the Cheap

We are really lucky to live in a time when mass production of common items is so plentiful.

As a result, bargain prices and bargain stores are everywhere.
Dollar stores in particular, will become your best friend, at least in the beginning. They offer most of what you need to get started. Let's list some of the items available for your immediate use.

Let's start with the *dollar stores* first.

1. Multi-packs of disposable paint brushes in various sizes, from 1" to 3" or 4" increments. It is exactly what you need. Cost: $1.00
2. Masking tape. 2" or 3" width is good enough. Cost: $1.00
3. Paint scraper (used to scrape mold, fungus, gum, etc. from painting surface). Cost: $1.00
4. Cleaner/degreaser: (any brand will do, but you'll usually find a brand name like "Spic & Span"). cost: $1.00
5. Long ruler or edger for straight lines. Cost: $1.00

Minus out the cost of anything listed that you already have. You probably have an old ruler and paint scraper already. Combined with a few household items, like clean cloths or a box-cutter or sharp knife, you are almost fully supplied with the "equipment" side.

1. Home Depot   2. Lowe's   3. Ace Hardware   4. True Value Hardware stores.

All of the above mentioned stores will have different bargain prices, so shop around for the best price. All four stores will serve your paint needs.

1. Black spray paint You only need one can of flat or semi-gloss black spray paint to start. Cost: $.97 to $1.09 depending on which of the four stores you go to.

2. One can of flat or semi-gloss white spray* paint. If your first time out is with a can of white spray paint, you can actually buy fewer brushes starting out. Cost:$.97-$1.09

3. Stencils. One pack of 3" alpha-numeric stencils. Cost: $2.49 to $3.49, again, depending on which store you purchase from. Also, you will want to replace these with higher quality templates as soon as possible. Many banner and sign shops carry the permanent templates made to order.

As you can see, it is truly possible to make money with as little as $10.00 to start with. This is why we call it a "$10.00" venture.

*Note: Most larger stores have an "OOPS!" rack. You can sometimes find comparable types of white paint for as little as $5.00 per gallon . . . well worth it if you can afford it.

II

Lot Painting

A. Small to Medium Parking Lots

Painting parking lots is another way to make a good amount of money in a relatively short time. Just for driving around your own neighborhood, you can probably spot all the lots from businesses and shops, gas stations, etc. that could use a fresh coat of paint.

The wear on ground painted objects like parking lane stripes, directional arrows, disabled parking lanes and the adjacent striped, walkway, is pretty constant. We've all seen them . . . faded and worn out. I noticed it too one day. A small church parking lot! Well, since I'm not shy and I'm always willing to simply ask for the business, I went inside and spoke with two gentlemen who were Deacons of this church. I immediately offered to repaint the lane stripes, including a "reserved" stencil in the minister's parking space, a handicap parking lane w/adjacent walking lane and 2 arrows near the driveway entrance (entrance and exit).

I had no real idea what I should charge for this service so, I grossly undercharged a flat-rate for the job at $125.00. I figured the relatively small lot would only take a few hours, at most. It actually took about 6 hours as I did not consider that I had to prep it first by running a wire brush over all the designated painting areas, and then clean it up. That's when I realized how versatile my wooden broom or mop handle and that bottle of "Fantastic" spray cleaner had become. It allowed me to interchange from brush to broom to roller. (It also made me realize the limits and time constraints of painting alone).

Over time I learned to plan my paint pattern for each lot for the fastest completion time and was able to start taking the slightly larger, mid-sized lots, of the type you see at some mom & pop stores, deli's, auto-shop lots etc. Again though, I started out with just the bare-bones equipment to do that "*first*" lot.

B. Starting up—Minimal Supplies & Equipment

The most noticeable difference between painting curbs and painting parking lots, is that you are stationary instead of traveling up and down the street. A nice change of pace . . . . you are working within a time-frame that includes a fixed price. Meaning you know *exactly* how much money you're going to make. You will need a lot more tape and more paint too. Also, some of what you purchased or used for curb addresses can also be used to help paint a small to medium sized parking lot as well. You get to use the *letters* of your stencil set. Words like "reserved", "customer parking only", limited 30 minute parking, fire-lane, no parking, do not block, keep clear, etc.

If it is a small lot, most often the owner will offer to provide the paint you need in exchange for a reduced or labor-only price. If not, then you need to purchase about 2 gallons of exterior flat or semi-gloss white, 1 gallon of safety yellow, 1 quart of rich blue enamel, 1 gallon of fire engine red, 1 gallon of flat or semi-gloss black and a 25 foot tape measure. About $100.00! Some of which you'll get back during billing. You may not use every color mentioned, but unless you know what the owner wants, you need to at least have these colors in stock. If you do know the colors your customer wants, then you can buy *only* those colors needed, greatly reducing your out of pocket expenses. Be sure to check the "oops" rack at any hardware store you visit.

You will literally tape your lane lines, arrows, boarders, etc. A 3" roller head and handle will work great once attached to the long broom or mop handle. Lane stripes can be either 3 or 4 inches wide and you can buy roller-heads of either length. As a thought, most **pawn shops** carry a good selection of gas powered lane stripers, at a ridiculously low price. After your first lot, or 2, you may want to invest in one. Sometimes, they're less than $50.00. Consider, that if you do buy a lane striping machine, depending on the model, you may be stuck buying spray cans of paint adapted for striper use. The cheaper models are manually driven, so a good eye for walking a straight line is helpful.

C. Lane Stripers, Spacing and Rollers

Lane lengths should be standard (20 Feet), especially when it's a small lot. Generally, the average vehicle in the United States is up to 20 feet long. Lately however, with the advent of smaller, more fuel efficient vehicles, you gain some flexibility in the length of your lanes. Shorter lanes, around 16 to 18 feet long will usually suffice. Just be sure to stencil "compact" in the shorter spaces.

It is important to maintain the proper *width* of your lanes too.

The average width of most parking stalls is about 8 ½ feet. Some locations are going a bit wider, due to the width of some popular vehicles like the "Hummer" or trucks with dual wheels on the rear.

A little precision is required here. Your lines whether vertical or angled, **must** be straight and even. Be sure to measure the length of each lane-line and mark it. Then, check your measurements. If you find your numbers changing for each lane, then you have an uneven lot. The beauty of lane painting is, if you screw up you can black it out and start again, with only a little time lost.

Bump-stops are painted white or traffic yellow, depending on the owner's preference. Some shops you solicit will also have speed bumps of varying thicknesses. They are usually yellow-striped using safety yellow paint. Safety poles are common to many lots these days. They're painted yellow or red mostly.

Lane stripers, as mentioned, are a way to really speed up the job. You can do 4 lane stripes for every 1 painted by roller. If there are a lot of lanes to be painted, this will make the job go very fast indeed.

The catch? A trade off! You see, it is a very thin coat of paint, which can fade or wear out *very* quickly. A second and third coat may be needed in those areas of really heavy vehicle traffic. Painting using a roller will give you a much thicker coating. A second coat is normally not necessary when using a roller. It takes a lot longer, but it will also **last a heck-of-a-lot** longer too. Striper machines come in a variety of sizes and extras. The base model will cost very little, but is one-dimensional in its function. If you can go just one step above the base models, your striper will have additional functions like a swing nozzle for painting the sides of perimeters, boarders, edges, sides of curbs, islands, etc. Rollers work too, only you're physically doing it. I find that doing 1 or maybe 2 lots using rollers is okay, but more than a couple of times makes it a tedious undertaking.

D. Flat rate or Hourly?

Starting out, simply flat-rate. Look at the lot, is it full of unfilled pot-holes? Is the asphalt so faded you need to lay a strip of black for each lane to enhance your white or yellow lane stripe? Has dirty engine oil and other vehicle fluids soaked in your painting areas? Is there greenery, shrubs or brush overhanging or overlapping into and onto the areas you need to paint? Consider the added time it would take to remedy any of these scenarios.

Assuming you've taken a small or medium sized lot, Ask the owner if he wants to patch up his lot and have the additional amount tacked to his bill, or if he wants to buy the one or two buckets of patch-fill and just pay the additional labor instead. In addition, if the pot-hole or severe crack is in your line of fire (crosses your painting lane), you may have to stop long enough for it to harden. The same is true if you have to degrease any surface areas that have to be painted because, after you degrease, you'll have to wash it off and wait for that section to dry. It should not stop you from painting other areas in the mean time. I recommend a flat rate for the small lots because you can start at one price and allow the *owner* to tack on the additional services themselves. If you do decide to go hourly, additional price could range from 100.00 to*250.00 max.*(includes all paint and supplies). If you flat rate, time no longer becomes a factor and you can always add to your price on any additional work needed

E. By the stripe or Square Footage

How does one arrive at the right price for a lot? The two most common methods are by square footage or by the number of items painted. Even if you are not good at math, don't worry, you don't have to be . . . that's what calculators are for. A 250 ft lot equals 1000 sq ft. If you charge by the square footage, your price could look like: .51cent per sq ft x 1000 ft = $510.00. A fair price for the size of the lot. Generally, that .51 cent includes supplies, material and labor. Almost every business owner or manager I've met knows his or her lot's size. If your client is providing the paint you need, you price may include labor and some materials but obviously, not supplies. Your price per sq ft. reduces to perhaps: .39psf x 1000 = $390.00.

*Note: Remember, observe the surroundings before quoting any prices. Pay attention to incoming and out going traffic. If a really busy location, a second coat on selected areas must be considered in your estimate. Look for problem areas, like heavy cracking, pot holes or root protrusion, severe mold, etc. You want him/her to know that you performed a very thorough lot inspection and can include any of the above additional service needs in your price.

If you are thinking about charging by the number of items painted, that works well too. Each item has its price. Below is only an example of how item pricing can also equal a good price and good profit.

Let's say you counted all lanes and can now itemize your bill. Assume we are talking about the above lot example, you count a total of:

35 parking stalls with a total of 30 actual lane stripes, you charge $2.55 per stripe, which equals $76.50

6 directional arrows at $12.00 each equals $72.00

10 Wheel stops at $6.00 each equals $60.00

5 safety poles at $8.00 each equals $40.00

1 speed bump at $15.00 .... $15.00

30

1 50 foot Fire lane equals.. $46.50

Handicap parking emblem $42.00 .... $42.00

Curbs, boarders and perimeters at $125.00 .... $125.00

TOTAL.. $477.00

So as you can see, at the $510.00 rate, there is only a $33.00 difference between the 2 methods. You have to be the judge of which method is appropriate for whom. The danger in offering a price based on per item pricing, is after you make your quote, what if the prospective customer decides to cover the all paint and supplies needed? You would basically be forced into a flat-rate, labor only quote. Unless you really plan on going big-time and start bidding for supermarket or mall lots, you should be able to just about flat-rate all of your lot prospects.

III

Yard/Lawn Care

A. Got A Truck?

Having a truck can certainly widen the diversity of any hands-on venture you undertake. If a you have a van, pick-up, truck or even a station wagon, a whole new set of jobs open up to you.

Say you just painted the curb address of a resident and notice their yard could use some upkeep. You have the perfect opportunity to ask for additional business. Yard and lawn care are not necessarily synonymous with each other. Try to cover all jobs relating to the **exterior** of the home first. Like gutter cleaning or regular lawn care. If you spot dirty blinds through the window, you can offer to clean them for a single price for all the blinds in the house or "per room". No matter what additional work you get, a truck will make you very competitive, because you'll be able to carry everything you need, no matter which service they choose.

B. Start with a Weed Eater

I found that carrying a weed eater (hedge clippers and snips come in handy too) with you in the back of your car or truck can really come in handy. Sometimes people just want a trim around the edges of their lawn, driveway or walk-way. It keeps uneven, overgrown grass from looking *too* ragged. Offer to edge it up for them for say, $15.00 or so. If they have hedges or other type bushes, offer to shape them up and glean the ragged over-height small branches and twigs that may obstruct views or look uneven. Don't be afraid to ask for the business, after all, they're already customers and this *one* customer can become a *repeat* customer, whom you can schedule regular service times and really start to show your presence on the block and in the neighborhood.

C. Schedule Yourself for a 4 Day Work-Week

To help establish your "territory", you should continue to offer the variety of services mentioned here, to all you come into contact with. Make your self available at least 4 days a week. You need the flexibility to schedule several homes and functions daily. Your goal should be to do a minimum number of client homes everyday of your 4 day week. 2 to 4 jobs daily can result in a paycheck that's worth your efforts. Let's say there are 5 homes on a street that want their grass cut every 2 weeks. 2 of the homes could be every other Tuesday, say the 1st and 3rd Tuesday of each month, and the other 3 homes would be the 2nd and 4th Tuesday of each month. Repeat this same type of scheduling for each of the four days you chose as your "work-week", until you've taken as much work as you want to handle.

D. Time and Profit

Time and profit are of paramount importance as you ponder the option of procuring add-on sales to existing or new customers. If time and profit are your concern, try to combine these two, let's meld them. A different approach may be to not worry about time and profit as much as *"timing your profits"*.

Continuing the model of a 4-day work week, keep building your lawn care business until you've reached your point of satisfaction and decide how best to set-up your payment due dates; Monthly? Bi-monthly? Quarterly? Most gardening or lawn care operators charge monthly. It's good to have regularity and consistency when dealing with the public. Besides, this gives you more *lump-sum* payments at the end of each month or billing cycle. Let's say you have 16 customers who get their lawns cut regularly every 2 weeks, 8 lawns are serviced on the 1st and 3rd week of each mo. And the other 8 are serviced on the 2nd and 4th weeks of each month. That is steady and regular work for 4 days a week, every week. If you charge the usual 55.00 mo. average Fee, that gives you $880.00 mo as supplemental income* . . . . more if you take on a partner. That's timing your profits. Basically you give yourself a once monthly pay day. $880.00 a month is not enough by itself but, added to other services you should be offering by now, you can turn a single task into a regular repeat customer and provide a source of consistent income.

*Assumes due-date for each client is the same.

E. Why not "pay upon completion" instead?

A fair question! Quite simply, there will be *plenty* of occasions for you to accept "pay upon completion" arrangements as you will have many different customer preferences to deal with. Some people are a little paranoid and don't want to be listed on anything, including someone's regular route. Some people are cautious and would rather pay by cash or check as they go, because they don't want to commit, and some people will like the convenience of monthly billing/collections. So, don't limit your pay options too narrowly. People will say no sometimes because there is a *lack of payment options*.

And remember, **you want *repeat* business**, pay upon completion gives you money now, but does not give your customer a sense of commitment like billing cycles do. **The idea is to lock them in or, at least have them feel obligated to continue with *your* services above all other competitors.** Believe me, there will always be one or two cash-only customers on every block you do. If you practice a pay upon completion preference, you will have to expect an *inconsistent* customer base. Some weeks they'll say okay and other weeks they may "let it go 'till next time". That's the negative side of P.U.C. (pay upon completion).

IV

Debris Removal

A. Alone, Repeat Business Could Be Slow

Debris removal is another low-cost venture. Problem is, it is difficult to *maintain* a debris removal service with *regular* clientele. You are constantly on the move scouting out potential sites to solicit. If you are offering only debris removal, business could be slow. Because it is so easy, a lot of other guys with trucks take advantage of such an easy market, especially when it comes to storefronts or lots. Not just stores, but other industries that have parking lots or simply large ground space that need regular maintenance. A good plus about debris removal in industrial districts is, the wooden pallets from big-rig deliveries are recyclable for cash. Pallets are part of the debris problem for many shipping companies and distributorships.

If you're wondering if such businesses already have a service of this type or a department within the company that performs regular maintenance, or ground-keeping services, the answer is that most companies find a greater advantage in using outside contractors and vendors to handle external building esthetics. Your focus would actually shift from the residential areas to commercial or industrial locations. You are simply looking for any location showing some signs of neglect or accumulation of junk and debris near the trash area of their property. Most recycling companies do not pick-up wooden pallets.

Dump fees are a regularly included charge for anyone in the debris hauling business. On the plus side, it takes almost nothing in the way of overhead to get started. A truck of fair capacity or a hitch for attaching an empty trailer bed will be all that you need to get started. Along with some good gloves, and a willingness to clean up open areas, it could be a way to generate cash without spending anything more than maybe a little gas money. Rates are flexible too, depending on the type of debris you are hauling, you can charge for higher dump fees for toxic materials like silicone motherboards or old computers and servers. Check the dump rates for recyclables, perishables, steel and concrete and general trash. The rates are different for each.

B. Sub-Contracting specific types of loads

You can specify the types of debris you want to haul by the type of companies or businesses you contract to. If a large apartment complex ask you to come by once a week to remove all furnishings left behind by departing residents, you have to be willing to haul couches, chairs, old mattresses, etc. but not necessarily refrigerators or freezers. If it's a Chemical company, you can specify "empty containers only" You should specify the parameters of your hauling preferences by listing those items that can be included in your initial arrangement.

C. Easy but physical

Debris removal and hauling is easy, "no-brainer" work, but can be very physical depending on what you are hauling. Remember you are *manually* picking up trash and debris and objects. Some things may weigh quite a bit, and it's best to get help rather than to strain your self. This is especially true if you are removing concrete or other demolition type debris. Wear the proper back brace and bend your knees when lifting. Wear eye protection and dust mask when dealing with dusty air or other minute bits of stuff floating around in the air. Don't handle anything toxic or caustic without properly protecting your self with gloves and coveralls. Invest in a cheap Haz-Mat list. (Hazardous Materials List)

D. Best to combine this service with . . .

As stated earlier, alone, repeat business could be slow . . . . unless you combine it with another service like gutter cleaning or yard service and grounds keeping. If you have the 4" letters or larger, you can try to include some other services, like advertising weekly specials on store front glass. Stencil prices for sales specials, color code parking areas or number parking spaces (yellow stripe for limited parking or white for 2 minute load/unload) etc.

Be inventive, be creative, be ever on the look out for more work at every company or place of business you visit. Offer car washing services for employees if permissible, use everything you have in your personal experience arsenal to accomplish your expansion of services.

V

Gutter Cleaning

A. Another Low or No-Cost Start-Up

This is another job that really is low cost to start. Assuming you have a good sales attitude and already have some type of vehicle, all you need is a ladder (at least 20-feet long) and a water hose. (obviously, don't accept jobs that exceed the height of your tallest ladder).

As long as you have a nozzle that's adjustable to a high velocity stream, you're set to go!! That's it!!

This is a great seasonal money-maker that cost practically nothing to start but, can result in permanent routes and clientele.

B. Easy Work with Some Minor Risk

Gutter cleaning is fairly easy, but tedious. There are some **liabilities** to bear in mind also. You run a few small risks of "no-charge" repairs when doing gutters, like rusted clamps and attachments that break off while you are cleaning it, or a ladder that slips or a hose that slaps a glass pane too hard. These little hazards go with the territory unfortunately.

Keep this in mind when accepting a request for service. Because worn parts are common on gutter clamps and other restraints, _a good inspection of the entire gutter tract is always first_.

Inspections are your friend. It shows professionalism. Inspections help increase your asking price with additional work, informs your customer of deteriorating portions of their gutter system and protects you from claims of damage. Removal and replacement of worn clamps and such can add extra $$$ to your estimate. (This does pre-suppose of course that you can change a clamp).

It might be beneficial to keep a standard and phillips screwdriver handy, along with some various size clamps and retainers.

C. Can be easily combined with another service

This is a service that works great in combination with another service. Take debris removal, if you are prospecting in commercial or industrial locations, then combining different services can only increase your profits and reputation. Gutter cleaning and debris removal together is a good combination that can be scheduled once quarterly, semi-annually or annually. Obviously, you'll have to concentrate on building your clientele if you plan on any long-term profits. Almost any exterior service you can think of can be incorporated into your regular gutter cleaning schedule. This is especially true if clearing land or acreage becomes part of the scenario.

D. Arrange Regular Cleaning/Clearing Schedules

Regularly scheduled service is pretty easy when it comes to gutter cleaning. It's the one service where scheduled service rarely interferes with anything else you may have going.

There are long gaps in between service. You will find most businesses have it done only once or twice a year, unless leaves and other plants are in such abundance as to necessitate more frequent maintenance visits.

It becomes crystal clear, that many, many clients are needed to fill the gaps in service times. Scheduled regular service calls should be 3 to 6 months apart, on average, per customer. Home owners may only have it done annually. For land and/or acreage clearing, growth cycles will usually determine the schedule for you.

Let's say you've picked up 5 clients in mid-May, 4 businesses and 1 home owner. All 4 companies want their gutters cleaned every 6 months regularly, and the 1 home owner needs his done every 3 months.

You have just secured income for the month of November since all four businesses will be billed simultaneously. The home owner will be a good reminder and guide as to which month to try and fill next. Your goal is to work to fill the NEXT 3-to-6 months ahead with new, scheduled customers.

E. Takes time, but well worth it.

Scheduling a company for just 2 or 3 visits per year may have you wondering if this is a good idea or fit for you.

Look at it like this; every customer you get *now*, (and the money too), will repeat its same cycle of profit at least twice a year for you. A February client, is also a **guaranteed** July client . . . . A March client is a **guaranteed** September client . . . . and so on . . . . You can actually fill enough of each month to work only 10 or 15 days a month if you stagger your service dates properly.

10 or 20 customers can yield 20 or 40 checks . . . in your name, at least twice a year!! Your prices would no doubt be based on the size of the entire gutter track so, you could be charging 50 or 60 bucks for small residential homes, and upwards of 100 to 400 (or 500 bucks + for the larger industrial or commercial buildings).

Businesses are the fastest way to accomplish this goal of filling your calendar. Home owners are good if you can find tracts of homes located in heavily wooded areas or high top trees, especially pine trees. Always pay particular attention to any developed areas having dense greenery or forestation.

VI

Parts Retriever—Junk Yards can make you money!

A. If you don't mind getting dirty . . . .

If you don't mind getting dirty, then positioning yourself at or near the entrance of a parts recycler is where you want to be. Sometimes, you just need a little extra cash without the need to actually start a "business" per se. Plus, your true "start-up" cost is the price of admission into the yard.

There are a heck-of a-lot of people who will go to a junk-yard to get auto or truck parts in order to save some serious money. Thing is, they sometimes are not exactly dying to pull these parts on their own. They have no problem shelling out 10, 15 or 20 dollars if it will save them the trouble. The bigger the part, the more you can charge. The more difficult to remove a needed item, the more they are willing to pay.

You sell yourself as a "parts retriever". The title describes exactly what you do. You will pull any part desired by a patron and charge him/her according to the part itself and the degree of difficulty in removing the part. A lot of do-it-yourself mechanics use this type of hustle quite often to supplement their income. If you are handy with a wrench, grab your toolbox and post your self at an auto-recycler near you. If more recyclers are in the vicinity, you can have several locations in rotation.

B. Auto Parts Knowledge is Critical

Not to overstate the obvious but, a basic or fair knowledge of auto parts is critical to a successful day. If you cannot figure out how to remove a part and wind up damaging it instead, (and cannot find another) the result can be a bad reputation real quick.

The good news; you're at a junk-yard, who cares how you get the part out, as long as you don't ruin it doing so. Remember, you are only *removing* the item, not *installing* it. If it's not the right part, you can leave it where it is and move on. Someone else will thank-you anonymously for the removed item.

*A fun "also" to add in here is; For each vehicle you intend to check or remove parts from, check the back seat, if it has one, for change that's worked its way down the cushion. I dropped a washer one day and while digging in the rear seat for it, I kept pulling up coin change instead. It was about $2.60something. I started to look for junkers with back seats still in them and lo'and behold, I winded up with about $12.00 in change . . . . .enough for lunch and then some.

As long as you have the proper tools, you can pick up 6 to 10 customers a day at varying prices at several different lots. The greater your knowledge of automotive, or prowess at removing parts, the greater variety of retrievals you can accept.

Time is money so, you want to move quickly. Only one customer can be serviced at a time, but you can take several *orders* at a time and stack your customers. Give estimates or times for them to meet you at the cashiers booth or snack area. You will find it more productive to stay inside and do 2, 3 or 4 retrievals at a time, instead of single trips.

C. Year Round Opportunity

My sincere sympathies if you live in a cold-weather state, but this is something that you can do year-round. Nearly every "pull-your-own" type of junk-yard is outdoors, so winter can be especially brutal on your hands if you have to deal with extreme cold while handling *metal* tools.

Parts retrieval is not confined to any season. That is good news to all us week-end entrepreneurs. Business can be especially good in winter . . . . for obvious reasons. It gets pretty darn cold out there and nobody really wants this type of dirty job in frigid conditions. If you can handle lousy weather conditions, be it snow, rain or heat, then this can give you a steady stream of "less hardy" folks who will gladly pay you for your retrieval services. You might almost consider this "peak season". Be sure to keep sufficient lubricants with you because metals will contract and expand under extremes of hot and cold.

D. You may need to talk with Junk-Yard owner/mgr

Some junk yards are free to enter and some charge a fee, with in & out privileges. Some lots charge an additional separate amount for parts exchange privileges to protect you from being stuck with the wrong part. That's really worth the extra charge because there is usually no returns, refunds or exchanges on junk-yard parts although some yards will allow exchanges only.
At many yards, there is a table or inspection area for you to compare parts before making the final purchase, but not always.

It is important for you to know the policy at each junk-yard you visit. If it is free to enter, then they more than likely do not accept returns and all sales are final. Because of the "all sales final" policy, these type of yards generally have an area for you to compare parts before buying.

If they charge admission, then they probably have a return policy that **excludes** anything electrical, and a separate, per item "parts exchange slip" for optional purchase. These facilities generally do not have an inspection area or table, just cashiers. Last are the junk-yards that have employees to service customers. These type of set-ups are of no help to you. They already have parts pulled and shelved and if the part requested is *not* readily available, they send an employee to go pull the part while you wait. Unless you are planning on asking for a job there, move on, the income potential is *zero.*

Once you've found a location you are comfortable with, ask to speak with the owner or manager of the facility and ask if it's okay to offer your services to arriving patrons. It's pretty much up to the owner/mgr. Most managers really don't care as you may see several competitors at the same location.

Some managers may feel they could lose out on additional sales because the *customer* is not browsing around themselves and possibly seeing other items which may have slipped their minds. This does not happen very often though, truth is, a lot of customers ask *you* to see if you can find something else they may be looking for and still other customers will simply accompany you and pick-up additional parts browsing around while you're working.

VII

Path-Maker
(snow state residents only)

A. If it snows in your state or area . . . .

Those of you who live in cold weather states or at least, *seasonally* cold weather states, can add this chilly gem to your service menu. When it snows, it is an opportunity for some limited quick cash. A little gas powered snow-blower is handy, if you happen to have one but, all you need is a simple aluminum snow shovel or even an ordinary shovel and you're off and running. This is really great in residential neighborhoods, and even better when there are a lot of seniors on the block. If you are young or reasonably healthy, this should be a good workout for you. Persons with heart conditions of **any** type should consult their doctor first. If you have any respiratory conditions, use good judgment, decide if you should do this, take breaks and pace yourself accordingly. This is simple, easy work, but increasingly physical over time.

B. Paths and Driveways

Going door to door can really pay off when you see 3 or more inches of snow on the ground. In residential neighborhoods, offering to shovel a path from the sidewalk to their door or stairs or driveway will keep you quite busy as long as the snow last. Obviously, this is one job that is <u>totally</u>

weather dependant, but while it last, it's a free-for-all for entrepreneurs. Have options to offer potential customers like, $9.00 for a path or maybe a bargain $15.00 for the entire sidewalk. The deeper the snow, the more attractive your offer sounds and the greater likelihood they'll accept. You can adjust your prices as the depth of the snow dictates. Path and driveway offers should not be limited to just residential; **if conditions allow for safe driving,** solicit businesses as well. They do not want any of their customers falling or slipping either, for a variety of reasons. Use common sense here, don't bite off more than you can chew. Don't attempt to service a really large business or facility if you are not equipped for it. Shoveling snow is hard work, snow has weight and is heavy. You can physically over do it. Stick with homes and small to medium sized businesses. You will find the speed at which you can finish paths and driveways, per customer, will allow you to maximize your time for the most profit possible. How fast you complete each job is a factor of your own health and stamina. So pace yourself. Remember, the work is easy, but physical.

C. Sand or Salt?

After clearing away the snow on your path, a good sprinkling of sand or salt on your completed work is a very good idea. It helps prevent falls and slipping, tremendously. It also helps keep the snow from building up again. Where Rock-salt will help prevent the snow from building up too soon, sand will give greater grip and traction. So, which one to use? Both! Once you've combined a bag of sand with a bag of rock-salt, you'll have a combination that will go further than either the sand or rock-salt alone. Use it sparingly, but don't be stingy. It's not critical to have a little rolling seeder or spreader to sling the sand and/or salt. You can do it by hand. If you want start out with the sand only, it's usually around $6.00 or $7.00 dollars for a 50-pound bag. The rock-salt is a buck or two more.

There will not always be a need to use either sand or salt. Most times on T.V. and/or radio, weathermen will forecast how much snow is expected to accumulate for a given time period. That bit of news can help you plan for how much sand or salt to have available, if any. Rising temperatures can save you sand and salt usage, time and money, but it also signals the end of your run.

D. Business or Residential?

Either choice is good.
Home-owners are easier to get, but businesses pay more.

Choosing businesses though, has its challenges;

1. A lot of managers will have an employee do it.

2. The property owners may have already contracted with another company.

3. Some places have invested in a snow-blower to keep on the premises.

4. Some businesses will not even bother to open.

That's the down side of it.

The good news is the smaller the business the greater your chances of securing said business. Not a lot of people look at just the little stores and shops. It could actually be very profitable because you can piecemeal each business or have each contribute a percentage of the total bill to have maybe their entire side of their strip or block done. This also helps you establish a rapport with local businesses that could generate additional services.

This is oversimplifying obviously, but the point has been made; taking advantage of snowfall, whether predicted, expected or spontaneous can result in some immediate cash earnings and good interaction between you and many local merchants. It's a nice introduction of your versatility, especially when you can offer other services to all the merchants you approach.

VIII

Blind Cleaning Service

A. An Unsaturated Market

This is another great little venture that can really grow to become a source of steady long-term income. There are not enough blind cleaning service companies out there, by comparison to the thousands upon thousands of homeowners, apartment dwellers and small businesses. This is a market that is not yet saturated and a good opportunity for a low-cost start-up. I actually picked up several dozen customers just from asking about it after I came to collect from painting their curb addresses.

If you can get a couple of poles or racks of either fixed height or that can extend upwards, you can make some really good money cleaning Venetian blinds. Whether vertical or horizontal, *nobody* likes to clean blinds, especially housewives and homemakers. This is one job that nearly everybody in the household will procrastinate doing.

If you have ever tried to handle Venetian blinds, you know how flexible and awkward they can be to handle. It is easy to damage or bend some of the blades. If that happens, you have to hope a few spare blades are around as they usually cannot be straightened out to any degree of *esthetic* satisfaction.

B. Excellent steady income as clientele builds

Blind cleaning is a repeat service. Every customer that has their blinds cleaned will be open to return dates or regular cleaning schedules. Your prices should be structured on the regularity of house visits and number of blinds per dwelling. If your price is reasonable enough, (doing a few blinds will let you gauge how much you should charge) you will see this client regularly 3 or 4 times a year. Do not cheat yourself by going **too low** on your price. You do not want to agree to clean 5 sets of blinds for 30.00. When given a specific number of blinds, be sure you know what *size* the blinds are first. A small, kitchen window blind can be a 10.00 item, but a panoramic living room pane with 10 foot vertical blinds is an easy 45.00+ alone. Check the various sizes in each room or window and total your average to a fixed price for your customer. If you can keep your prices at or around 100.00, you will probably get the repeat business. Of course, if you are dealing with a very large house or a lot of blinds, then adjusting your price to fit the job only makes sense.

Businesses have much greater gaps in scheduling than residential. Home-owners are the fastest way to accumulate clientele. This is why I tie most of these start-ups to curb painting. Again, a curb customer already has a dialogue with you and they will engage in conversation with you. After the curb is painted is the best time to inquire about additional services. You will find many receptive prospects who are genuinely interested.

C. Equipment is Fairly Inexpensive

There's nothing expensive about a simple rack . . . or even 2 poles stuck in the ground with a crossbar. As long as you can hang, raise and lower your horizontal blinds, you can quickly clean them. Vertical blinds are individually detached from the upper slide rail, and each slat is laid out for cleaning, usually on the front or back lawn or yard. A short, step ladder for removing and hanging the blinds is necessary.

Ordinary household cleaners will work very well. Spic & Span, Fantastic, Lysol, Mr. Clean or any spray cleaner and degreaser will work just fine. Dollar store cleaning items are a good place to get larger quantities of spray cleaners. They carry not only off-brand or generic products, but you often find brand name spray cleaners too. A couple of plastic spray bottles are handy too. Sometimes you may want to combine bleach with a cheap spray cleaner and mix the solution yourself. Dollar stores also carry a variety of useful accessories, like cleaning cloths, bundles of rags, paper-towels, soft brushes, firm brushes, cleaning mitts, etc. An ordinary garden hose is all you need if cleaning outside. Your only cost may be just some cleaning products if you already have a small ladder.

D. Web-site or Flyers

A local web site can change your venture into a very busy business. Suffice it to say that many people reading this guide do not have a computer. If you do, you can drive local traffic and inquires your way with a slick web-site extolling the benefits of your service. If you have no idea how to do this, I recommend you read and study the potential of hosting a web-site. There are free web-sites you can get by going to freewebsites.com that will teach you all you need to know about creating your own web-site. Since it's free, take advantage of it and learn all you can about advertising on the internet. The internet is useful, but success is not automatic . . . you have to develop it just like anything else. It takes time to learn and understand the nuances of internet advertising and hosting. You may even decide its more trouble than its worth. But no decision is forthcoming unless you explore at least the possibility of a web-site.

This is where flyers may help. Many responders to this guide know their local community well enough to target just a certain area or neighborhood. That being said, one has to consider the cost of printing hundreds, if not thousands of flyers. Distributing the flyers is also a time consuming ordeal as well. The unfortunate statistic is a **1% response average** on flyer distribution. One out of ten is not a good average to deal with. That means at best, you break even on the money spent to print and distribute the flyers. Personally, I have tried flyers and would never use that method again. It did not generate the business I wanted so I continued to gather my customers through curb-painting. Your circumstances may be different, so do not let my bias of flyers influence you to the point where you won't even consider it. The only sure way to know if it works for you is to try it.

Print just a hundred or so flyers and see what the response time as well as the number of respondents are, before you make a decision. One plus in all this is, it does start your creative juices flowing and you get some practical experience in advertising to help you round out your business acumen.

IX

Fish & Pet Tank Cleaning

A. Another Unsaturated Market

Here is another unsaturated market for the more adventuresome souls among us.

This is the only start-up where you will exceed 10.00 in start-up cost.

Fish tank cleaning is an off-shoot of the better known "Aquatic Services" business. While not as wide-ranging as aquatic services, which can cover everything from your pet turtle tank to cleaning swimming pools, fish and pet tank cleaning is a specialty field limited to pet tanks and aquariums of all types and sizes. If you have ever cleaned a fish tank, you know how unpleasant and ugly algae build-up and cleaning can be. The advantage of F&PT cleaning, is you can charge a hell-of-a-lot less than the full service aquatic companies. Even if you expand into complete tank set-ups, your cost is moderate at worse. While there are other well established aquatic service companies out there, many of these same companies are also in the tank supply business as well, meaning higher operating cost, making their mobile aquatic services more costly.

Since you would not be buying a lot of equipment for the full range of aquatic services, at least not at first, your prices should be substantially lower than any aquatic service company's prices. Eco-friendly and safe cleaning solutions are very inexpensive. One bottle is 4.00 to 5.00 and will last for about 5 tank cleanings, depending on the size of the tank(s).

B. Minimal Equipment Requirements

Items like Algae scrapers, fish nets for capturing, glass polish, etc. are all very nominally priced items. While researching the most current prices of common equipment items, it seems prices are consistent at nearly all of the stores and distributorships. This is a business that can grow with loyal repeat customers but it will definitely cost much more than $10.00 to start if you want make sure you have everything you need to start cleaning tanks and aquariums. The plus side is, you will not just expand, but evolve. That means your service menu grows and grows until there is nothing about aquariums you cannot handle, including new tank set-up, filtration systems, netting, etc.

Minimally, you will need An Algae scraper (5.99), Lime-off (1.89), Aquarium cleaner (4.99), Aquarium wipes,(7.99) and a scoop-net (2.49). Less than $25.00 total. You could actually start with just the aquarium cleaner, scraper and net. To make sure I point you in the right direction, here are a few internet sites to check out for pricing, supplies, accessories and information.

Aquariumguys.com
Petsmart.com
Thatpetplace.com
Marinedepot.com

The exploration of products and equipment will encourage you to read about the function and proper usage of equipment and other devices, and with a little practice, turn you into an expert on the function and use of all things tank-related.

C. Appointment Only Option

Some Tank and Aquarium operators prefer to do business by appointment only. That is an entirely personal choice. Appointment only operators are those who have decided to dedicate only a specific number of days or hours per week to service clientele. Some because they work full-time and can only spare certain days and times, others because they only want to do this on a part-time basis or have not yet filled their calendar with enough customers to fill their target saturation point. Whatever the reason, it is an option you can entertain.

Some people think appointment only suggest the person is not fully dedicated to the industry and is not as knowledgeable as someone who fully invest their time into this business. While untrue, this is the perception some people have. Most callers who want service will set-up an appointment anyway, so it's really not a big deal to go a step further. On the positive side, setting appointments adds a personal touch that makes your customer feel a little special or like a preferred client. That's a great touch and will enhance your rapport with them on every visit.

D. Web-Site is best tool for new business

If you are computer savvy, a web-site is the best tool for garnering new customers. As with all the other start-ups listed here, the main bulk of your **first** batch of customers will come from **curb-painting**. As stated in the very beginning of this guide, any option you chose to explore has a great head start because you are already in contact with homeowners and dwellers.

If you want to experiment with the internet, I advise you wait until you have 15 or 20 repeat customers from your efforts while curb painting. That way, you already have a steady source of income and will have the time and money to slowly study the potential influx of new customers by using the internet. A web-site can bring in additional revenue for you because at some point, in addition to new F & PT customers, you will probably learn about adding affiliate programs that boost your income on a per-click basis.(per click means someone went to another site from your web page . . . . you get paid for that). I have included the web addresses to a couple of sites that offer free web-sites and free web-site hosting. It will instruct you on the way to use such a site to tailor your message or ad to your targeted audience.

It requires a lot of reading and studying but since it's completely free, I would encourage you to take advantage of these sites to learn if web-hosting and advertising on the Internet is for you.

<u>www.freewebsites.com</u>   or   www.yola.com

Even if you do not own a computer, surfing the web is pretty commonplace and most of us can at least do that. However, not everybody is *comfortable* with the internet as a profit making tool. This is a whole new level for many of us.

I know of several people who seem quite satisfied getting more add-on business from curb-painting and are very happy with the flow of customers they get from their face-to-face encounters. They've found their comfort zone. It is a personal choice each individual must decide for themselves.

X

Residential Window Cleaning

A. Low Cost Money-Maker

This was actually an accidental find. While collecting on a curb painting completion, the lady asked; "Do you do windows too"? half-jokingly. Thinking this is something I should say yes to, I replied in the affirmative and she took me on a talkative tour of her home to point out all the windows that had been neglected because she nor her husband were able to climb and stand on a ladder or stepstool for any appreciable amount of time, certainly not long enough to accomplish a proper cleaning.

I was shown about 7 ordinary-sized windows she could no longer comfortably reach. Flying blind, so to speak, I quoted $50.00 even for inside or outside only and $99.00 for both as an "introductory special". She took the $50.00 inside only deal. I set an appointment with her to return during the mid-week. This allowed me time to run to my favorite place to get a cheap, gallon bottle of window cleaner and a squeegee. Again, I spent less than ten bucks for the supplies I needed. You really don't need a ladder if have good garden hose, but at least a step-stool should be kept handy for the inside of the home. With the non-streaking cleaners and the various hose attachments you can get these days, outdoor window cleaning is almost painless.

The windows were relatively easy for a younger person to handle, so the strategy was to excite her into wanting more. (sometimes folks, you just have to play it by ear) Sure enough, after I posed a question to her regarding my return, if any, she was surprised I was willing to do so.

We arranged a monthly visit for all the out side windows only, for $90.00, (she insisted on a discount because she was a member of AARP, so rather than lose the entire sale, I relented).

It was mutually agreed that there would be no service during the Winter months.

I had just secured my first **residential** window customer. How suddenly the entire block began to look like a giant dollar sign.

In thinking about it, I slowly realized that I never really noticed window cleaners on *my block* . . . . .hmmm, no one else's either . . . .

B. Perfect Companion

As you may have figured by now, this is a ***great*** companion task for blind cleaning, yard/lawn care or even tied to a quarterly gutter cleaning. It makes a perfect companion. It gives you another avenue of profit from the same source.

The key here is _residential_ ! You can find or see commercial window cleaning services and people all day, but for homes, the commercial service companies can be a bit pricey. You still have to deal with negotiating with home owners as to the frequency of your service visits, prices and discounts, especially for seniors but, that goes with the territory. There is a certain satisfaction you feel when haggling over the number of visits a particular price may include. It means you've made the sale and now the details are being worked out.

Notice I do not recommend businesses. Unless you have already secured a few customers or at least, scouted an area you believe will be worth the effort, businesses can be a tough sell. Many of you will become discouraged and some will abandon the idea altogether. Plus, the commercial glass cleaning companies are highly competitive and mostly well established.

They don't often lose a client once they get one, and they're smart enough to secure a service contract for years.

As far as businesses go, if it's not a little Mom & Pop type store, securing long term commitments or at least occasional return visits may be very difficult.

If you are up to such a challenge, I salute you! The reward can be a great, long term service schedule, providing years of reliable income. Big-Risk = Big Reward.

The residential scene however, is truly different.

You can operate at a pace much less demanding than the industrial or commercial scenario.

You can build your clientele steadily through-out the season and beyond. The number of maximum customers though, should be considered carefully.

Some factors to ponder:

At what point is saturation reached within a given grid or area?

Can a lost customer, (moved, died, sold home) be replaced within the same area?

How does the standard architecture of each home affect the pricing and time-line for completing a home within a tightly scheduled time-frame. Does it have greater number of windows as compared to other homes on the block?

How many clients can I realistically maintain and how many do I *need* to reach a comfortable profit margin?

These are questions that will mostly be answered as you gain a better knowledge of how long it takes to complete each home. No doubt the per house completion rate will vary, some slightly, some greatly.

This is more important to gauge than you may suspect. Time management is ultimately tied to the number of completed homes in one quarter (90 days). Study the results of that first quarter.

Then, you will be able to better co ordinate how you combine your schedule for a certain day or area or type of home. Once a few months have passed, you will know to schedule a 2 hour job with two, 3 hour ones and such. Obviously, maintain some method to track the length of time for each home for the first couple of visits.

C. Add Screen cleaning

Adding an item like Window Screens can be an easy, easy way to increase your total ticket.

When quoting your prices be sure to say this includes the screens. Let them know you offer screen cleaning with any window that has one, because of the sheer amount of dust and other particles that accumulate and layer itself onto the screen surface and eventually blocks all the air from circulating. This allows you to have a justifiably higher price. The growing pain here is learning how to price each client's home. Trust me, it won't take long to figure out if you are charging too little.

Close

In closing, let me mention to all reading this guide, **please be sure to check local laws and requirements for operating a business within city and/or county limits.** Each municipality has its own ordinances. They do vary significantly from one area to the next.

There are licenses, permits, vendor applications, distributorships, etc. for you to check. Know the difference between them and do not be afraid to ask questions about which license or permit fits the type of start-up you intend to try. In most cases, a permit is all you need. The cost of permits vary from city to city, as do the rules that govern them.

Unless you plan to save all receipts and expenses to claim for the end of the year on your taxes, you should **perform a marketing test** for yourself. It also gives you a chance to perfect your script. A feasibility test is a couple of weeks of soliciting to see if the areas or grids you've selected produce the results you are hoping for. I would not apply for a permit or license until you have completed your evaluation.

Also, please remember that these suggestions are aimed at people who want to start something they normally would not be able to afford. It also requires no formal training, just a few customers is all you will need to learn how to do anything discussed here. **Curb painting is the key** that opens the many doors you have been reading about. Stay positive, it is the individual's own efforts that is the best guarantee of success and profitability.

Success to you all . . . .

www.ingramcontent.com/pod-product-compliance
Lightning Source LLC
Chambersburg PA
CBHW021916170526
45157CB00005B/2087